STEM CAREERS

SOFTWARE ENGINEER

by R.J. Bailey

Ideas for Parents and Teachers

Pogo Books let children practice reading informational text while introducing them to nonfiction features such as headings, labels, sidebars, maps, and diagrams, as well as a table of contents, glossary, and index.

Carefully leveled text with a strong photo match offers early fluent readers the support they need to succeed.

Before Reading

- "Walk" through the book and point out the various nonfiction features. Ask the student what purpose each feature serves.
- Look at the glossary together. Read and discuss the words.

Read the Book

- Have the child read the book independently.
- Invite him or her to list questions that arise from reading.

After Reading

- Discuss the child's questions. Talk about how he or she might find answers to those questions.
- Prompt the child to think more. Ask: Do you know anyone who works as a software engineer? What projects has he or she been involved in? Do you have any interest in this kind of work?

Pogo Books are published by Jump!
5357 Penn Avenue South
Minneapolis, MN 55419
www.jumplibrary.com

Library of Congress Cataloging-in-Publication Data

Names: Bailey, R. J., author.
Title: Software engineer / by R.J. Bailey.
Description: Minneapolis, MN: Jump!, Inc., [2017]
Series: STEM careers | Audience: Ages 7–10.
Includes bibliographical references and index.
Description based on print version record and CIP data provided by publisher; resource not viewed.
Identifiers: LCCN 2017009865 (print)
LCCN 2017011262 (ebook) | ISBN 9781624965968 (ebook)
ISBN 9781620317198 (hardcover: alk. paper)
Subjects: LCSH: Software engineering–Vocational guidance–Juvenile literature. Computer programmers–Juvenile literature.
Classification: LCC QA76.758 (ebook)
LCC QA76.758 .B35 2017 (print) | DDC 005.1092–dc23
LC record available at https://lccn.loc.gov/2017009865

Editor: Jenny Fretland VanVoorst
Book Designer: Leah Sanders
Photo Researcher: Leah Sanders

Photo Credits: Getty: Colin Anderson, 5. iStock: Dragon Images, 1; gchutka, 5; vgajic, 6-7, 14-15; EXTREME-PHOTOGRAPHER, 8; Rawpixel, 10-11; Jacob Ammentorp Lund, 12-13; asiseeit, 18; mediaphotos, 19; Prykhodov, 23. Shutterstock: SGM, cover; In-Finity, cover; santapong ridprasert, 3; Africa Studio, 4, 9; Mr. Exen, 5; Dean Drobot, 16-17; Nestor Rizhniak, 20-21.

Printed in the United States of America at Corporate Graphics in North Mankato, Minnesota.

TABLE OF CONTENTS

CHAPTER 1

WHAT DO THEY DO?

Do you like computers? Would you like to use them to solve new problems? Become a **software engineer**!

Software tells computers what to do. It is why video games have great **graphics**. It is how your car's **GPS** knows the way home. It is why smart phones can do so much!

Computers have changed the world more than almost any other **technology**. But they can't do anything without people. People write software to make them work. These people are software engineers.

DID YOU KNOW?

A new **industry** is creating jobs for software engineers. What is it? Self-driving cars! These cars are safer. They save energy, too. Who knows? You may never have to learn how to drive!

CHAPTER 2

BUILDING SOFTWARE

Software engineers work closely with the people who will use what they make. First they ask questions. They find out what people need the software to do.

Design is the second step. They plan how the software will address people's needs.

The third step is creating the software. In this step, software engineers write **code**. These instructions tell a computer what to do. They use a **programming language**. There are many such languages. Each is suited to a different kind of task.

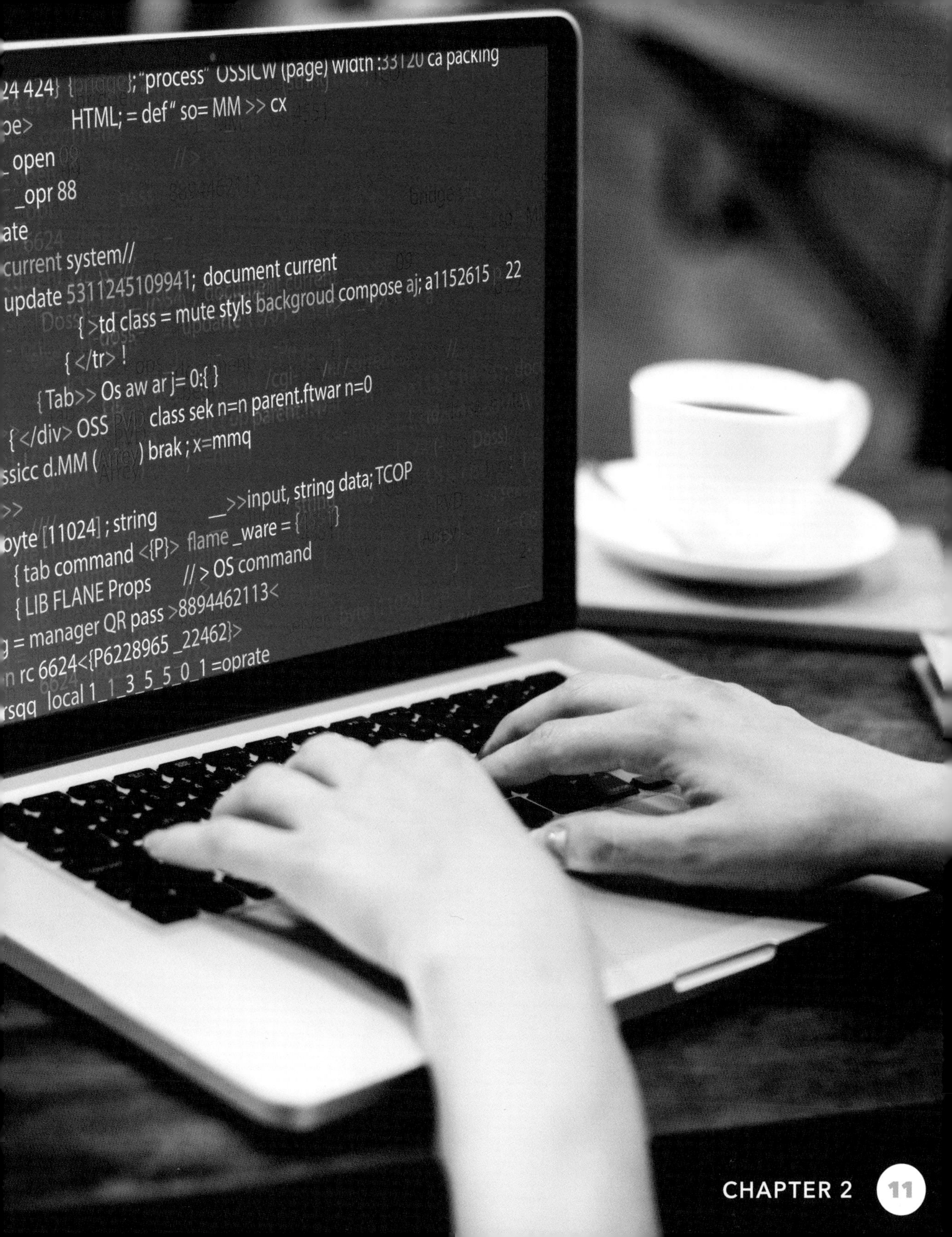

Now the software is written. What happens next? It is tested. Does it meet people's needs? Does it work correctly?

Sometimes software has problems that keep it from working correctly. These problems are called "bugs." Bugs can be hard to find. Software engineers work together to find the error. They review the code. They make changes. Then they test it again. They do this until they've fixed the bug.

After a successful test, the software is ready!

Finally, software engineers **maintain** software. Sometimes they change it, too. They might add new **features**. They might make it easier to use.

TAKE A LOOK!

Computers are everywhere. Look! All these things have computers in them!

CARS

GAMING SYSTEMS

AIRPLANES

CELL PHONES

WASHING MACHINES

DRONES

Software engineers work in offices. Some work in labs. They may travel to meet with customers. They often work nights or weekends to finish big projects. Because they work in teams, communication skills are important.

CHAPTER 3

BECOMING A SOFTWARE ENGINEER

Do you want to be a software engineer? Take computer classes. Do puzzles. They will help you learn problem-solving skills. Learn a programming language. Join your school's robotics club. It's a fun way to learn to code.

To work in the field, you'll want a college degree. Most people study software engineering or computer science.

It helps to get some job experience while in school. Many companies offer **internships**. This will give you real-world knowledge. It will make finding a job after college easier.

As a software engineer, you can shape the future. How? You can make software for self-driving cars. You can make exciting video games. You can help program new kinds of robots. The possibilities are endless!

ACTIVITIES & TOOLS

RUN A SIMPLE PROGRAM

Sort your classmates by height! Get three or more friends to stand in a line next to one another. Then follow these steps to run the program:

❶ Start with the pair of people on the far left.

❷ If the person on the left is taller than the person on the right, then swap the left and right person.

❸ Advance to the pair immediately to the right and repeat for each pair until you reach the end of the line.

❹ Go back to the leftmost pair and repeat these steps until no one needs to swap positions.

You have just run a sorting program! A computer would follow the same procedure if it were to sort numbers. There are many ways to sort. Some are faster than others. This one is called "bubble sort," because the largest object "bubbles" to the top.

GLOSSARY

code: The instructions a software engineer writes in a programming language to tell a computer what to do.

features: Interesting or important parts of something.

GPS: Short for Global Positioning System, a navigation system that uses satellite signals to determine location.

graphics: Pictures on a computer screen.

industry: A group of businesses that offer a particular product or service.

internships: Part-time jobs available to students in order to give them experience in a particular field.

maintain: To continue something without changing it.

programming language: A computer language that tells a computer or machine what to do.

software: The programs that run on a computer and accomplish certain functions.

software engineer: Someone who plans, builds, tests, and maintains software.

technology: Items of practical use created through the efforts of science and engineering.

INDEX

TO LEARN MORE

Learning more is as easy as 1, 2, 3.

1) Go to www.factsurfer.com

2) Enter "softwareengineer" into the search box.

3) Click the "Surf" button to see a list of websites.

With factsurfer, finding more information is just a click away.